Worcester Stacks Up

Firsts and Fun Facts

Jim
To a very very
good friend

CJ

PEOPLE
Sports
Art
Food
Health
PLACES
Education
Inventions

CJ Posk

Worcester Stacks Up: Firsts and Fun Facts
Copyright © 2012 by CJ Posk

This book is published and distributed by Lakshmi Books, LLC.

For information or to order bulk copies of this book, please contact the publisher at:

Lakshmi Books, LLC
P.O. Box 1205
Leominster, MA 01453

To report errors or additions, please send a note to books@lakshmibooks.com.

Visit the Worcester Stacks Up website at www.worcesterstacksup.com

Graphic design by JeanPaul Raymond
Cover concept by Liz Steele, design by Robin Wrighton and JeanPaul Raymond
Edited by Cheryl Cory
Layout and project management by Robin Wrighton
Printed by King Printing • www.kingprinting.com

Worcester Stacks Up / CJ Posk
November 2012

ISBN: 978-0-9848337-7-1

Library of Congress Control Number: 201293772

Printed in the United States of America

This book is supported in part by a grant from the Worcester Arts Council, a local agency which is supported by the Massachusetts Cultural Council, a state agency.

masssculturalcouncil.org

Dedication

In memory of Norma Feingold, educator and historian,
whose love of Worcester inspired me to write this book.

To Elaine Pajka, my reader and friend,
whose love of teaching and reading has guided me
through every page of this book.

To all the students who will have to see it to believe it,
including my own grandchildren,
Joey, Nicolas, Zachary, Avery and Max.

The city of Worcester, Mass. (downtown detail). Published by O.H. Bailey & J.C. Hazen, 1878. Norman B. Leventhal Map Center, Boston Public Library. ♥ Worcester City Hall.

Table of Contents

Worcester, Massachusetts and the surrounding area. Viewed from the south looking to the north. Taken from 3700 feet in a Cessna 150 airplane. 14 June 2006. © N. Wayne Hansen. ♥ Worcester City Hall.

So, Why Do We Celebrate

W hat started as an interest in reading about Worcester history somehow took on a life of its own and eventually evolved into this book for children and adults.

Once my curiosity was piqued, I couldn't stop collecting facts and tidbits about Worcester. My friend Elaine Pajka would read and I would type. I was amazed that the city was first in the nation in so many ways. The more I learned, the more I was convinced that I needed to share this rich history with others, especially children.

Eventually, these facts filled notebooks. The next logical step was to categorize all this information, and it was then that the book started to take shape. With the addition of graphics from JeanPaul Raymond, the book came to life. I was surprised we had collected so many firsts in the U.S.A. that took place in Worcester. What didn't fit in this category was too interesting to leave out, so I used this information to create the *Do You Know…?* question-and-answer section.

The publication of this book is my sincere attempt to foster in those who read it an appreciation of this city I call home. It was difficult to know where and when to stop researching. After many anxious days checking and rechecking my compilation of facts, and after many sleepless nights worrying about its authenticity, I drew my research to a close with a bibliography brimming and bursting with information.

This book is the result. I hope that readers learn as much as I did in putting this book together.

Have fun
C J

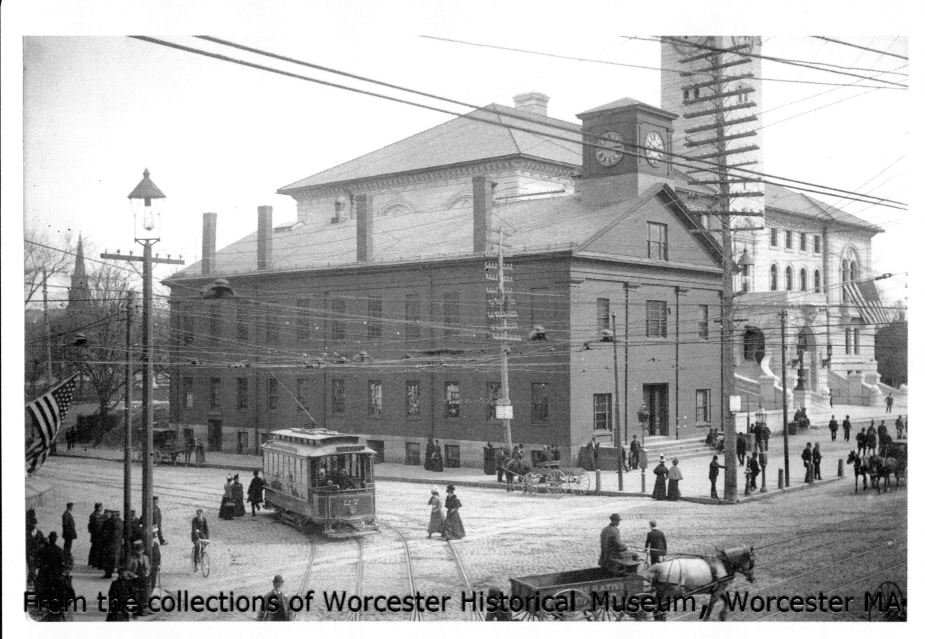

Old and New City Hall, 1898

Flag and Clock © Erb Photography

THE FIRST IN THE U.S.A.

It happened right here in Worcester!

Statue/City Hall © JeanPaul Raymond

Worcester was at one time an impressive industrial city. Today Worcester has transformed itself into an active and diverse center of modern industry, art and culture. It's now home to state-of-the-art healthcare and biotechnology industries, world-class colleges and universities, and some of the world's most innovative companies.

Worcester has long been a center of commerce, industry and education. It is also home to many of America's **FIRSTS**. Among other things, there have been great achievements in the arts, education, health and inventions.

SEE HOW WORCESTER STACKS UP

The First in Arts in the U.S.A.

The 1st American "believers"

in The Beatles were DJ Dick Smith and his Worcester audience. The volume of Fab Four requests, along with the group's popularity on the WORC music survey and charts, took off much earlier here than in the rest of the nation. In 1963, one of their songs, "I'll Get You," made the Top Forty locally. Not long after, the other side of the 45, "She Loves You," became so popular that Swan Records awarded Dick a gold copy of the record, calling him "America's first believer."

The 1st world-famous Smiley Face

was designed by commercial artist Harvey Ball in 1963 for State Mutual Life Assurance Company (located at 440 Lincoln St., now Hanover Insurance Group). He was asked to create a design to make the workers smile and was paid $45 for his contagious Smiley design. Does it make you smile?

The 1st pink flamingo

lawn ornaments were designed by Don Featherstone, a resident of Worcester. Union Products of Leominster contacted the Worcester Art Museum School looking for a student artist to join them and make their 3-D products. Don answered the call and went to work for them. He studied flamingos and created a clay sculpture of the famous bird. These attractive, tall, plastic pink flamingos are still being manufactured in Fitchburg by Cado Products, Inc. and are displayed on lawns all over the country. Look for Featherstone's signature to verify it's an original.

The 1st DJ credited

with discovering the song "The Lion Sleeps Tonight," by the Tokens, was Dick "The Derby" Smith, of WORC radio. He didn't think the song "Tina," the so-called A-side of a new Tokens record, had hit potential. But listening to the B-side, Dick immediately recognized a hit. His Worcester audience loved the song, which is now known worldwide, and has even appeared on the soundtrack to *The Lion King*.

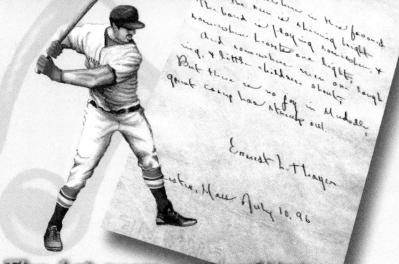

The 1st poem ever written

about "Casey at the Bat" was penned by Ernest Thayer in 1888. It might have been inspired by a classmate at Classical High School, Henry Casey. The last line of the poem is legendary: "But there is no joy in Mudville / Mighty Casey has struck out." Thayer wrote this poem when he lived on Chatham St. in Worcester and presented a handwritten copy of his poem to the Worcester Public Library in 1896.

The 1st person credited with mass-producing valentines

was Esther Howland. During the 1850s, she began making English-style valentines decorated with doves, lace, roses and sentimental messages in the attic of her family home at 16 Summer St. Howland employed several women and used an assembly line method of production. By 1874, she was using the name, "The New England Valentine Company," and her enterprise eventually grossed $100,000 per year. She was bought out by The George C. Whitney Co. of Worcester. Aren't these samples beautiful?

The First in
Education
in the U.S.A.

The 1st American Psychological Association

was organized by Dr. Granville Stanley Hall of Clark University on July 8, 1892. He was Clark's first president and the first person at Clark to hold a PhD in psychology, which he had received from Harvard in 1878.

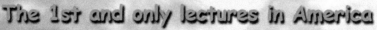

The 1st and only lectures in America

given by Sigmund Freud were held at Clark University from September 6-11, 1909. He delivered his "Five Lectures on Psychoanalysis" and later published them under the title "The Origin and Development of Psychoanalysis." Carl Jung accompanied Freud and also gave lectures.

The 1st American Psychiatric Association,

formerly known as the Association of Medical Superintendents of American Institutions for the Insane, was established in 1844 by Samuel B. Woodward. He was the first superintendent of the Worcester State Lunatic Hospital, the only hospital in the U.S. that Sigmund Freud visited when in America.

The 1st graduate school of geography

was opened at Clark University in the fall of 1921. Dr. Wallace W. Atwood, the president of Clark at the time, was director of this program.

The 1st Women's Classical Institution

that offered full classical and college courses for women was Oread Institute. It was founded by Eli Thayer in 1848.

The 1st university

in the country to offer only a graduate degree program was Clark University, at its founding in 1887. An undergraduate degree program was added in 1902.

The 1st college in the country

to offer a bachelor's degree program in robotics engineering was Worcester Polytechnic Institute (WPI). First offered in 2007, the program continues to attract many excellent students interested in this exciting technology.

The 1st doctorate in anthropology

in the U.S. was awarded at Clark University on March 9, 1892, to Alexander F. Chamberlain.

The First in Food
in the U.S.A.

The 1st to market a packaged pizza pie mix, tradition tells us, was Frank A. Fiorillo in 1952. This author can vouch for it. I opened the package, made the dough, poured the can of pizza sauce, and sprinkled the cheese. Best packaged pizza I ever tasted! Frank's first pizza stand was opened in 1947. It was bought out by Appian Way.

The 1st packaged rice pilaf was made by Hannah Kalajian. She started serving her Armenian-style rice pilaf at her husband's luncheonette counter. Kalajian started packaging the first 100% all-natural, kosher recipe with her husband George, and together they formed the popular Near East Food Products in 1962, marketing over 30 different varieties. Today, Near East foods are manufactured by Quaker Oats Company.

The 1st manufacturer of shredded wheat was

Shredded wheat... Mmmm

Henry Perky, an advocate of vegetarianism and healthy eating. Perky came to Worcester in 1892, and he began manufacturing shredded wheat in a shop at 57 Jackson St. in 1895. He also owned the former Oread Institute, where he served various creative dinners that showed how his nutritious ingredient could be used for every occasion. After twelve years, Perky moved the company to Niagara Falls and sold it. The company went on to become Nabisco Shredded Wheat.

The First in
HEALTH
in the U.S.A.

One of the 1st federally-licensed AIDS tests, approved by the FDA in 1987, was the rapid western blot test, developed by Worcester's Cambridge Biotech, formerly Cambridge BioScience Corp.

The first oral contraceptive pill

was developed in 1957 at the Worcester Foundation for Experimental Biology, located in the suburb of Shrewsbury. It was developed by Drs. Gregory Pincus and Min-Chueh Chang, and it was approved by the FDA and marketed in 1960. Over the years, the Pill has been shown to have many medical benefits for women. Pictured above is the original packaging.

The 1st bacteriological laboratory

was the Worcester Health Laboratory at 251 Belmont St./Skyline Drive. It opened its doors in 1885 at Worcester's City Hall and moved in 1936 to this Richardsonian Romanesque-style building. This was the first such public health lab in the country, and is the only remaining part of the larger Belmont Hospital Complex. It would be the perfect location to preserve and display Worcester's important contributions to medicine.

The 1st sewage disposal

using chemicals was instituted by Worcester in 1890 to clean up the polluted Blackstone Canal, opened in 1828.

The First in INVENTIONS
in the U.S.A.

The 1st successful envelope-folding machine

in the U.S. was built in 1853 by Dr. Russell Hawes, who lived on Salisbury St. The machine allowed three girls to produce 25,000 envelopes in ten hours.

The 1st steam calliope

was invented in Worcester in 1855 by Joshua Stoddard. This musical instrument combined the steam whistle with the musical scale. The keyboard is connected by wires to the valves and whistles. The calliope was popular at carnivals and circus parades, and it also appeared on trains and riverboats.

The 1st precursor to the modern typewriter was patented by Charles Thurber in 1843. In 1887, *Scientific American* magazine called his machine "the first American typewriter." Thurber said he invented the machine for the blind, the disabled, and those "nervous" about writing by hand. The surviving full-size example is owned by Worcester Historical Museum, located at 30 Elm St.

The 1st grinding machine was built in Worcester by the Norton Grinding Company in 1873. It could remove as much as three cubic inches of steel or chilled iron per minute. The company is now Saint-Gobain, located at One New Bond Street.

COATES' FACTORY ON CHANDLER S
GREW IN IMPORTANCE AND H
SALES AGENTS ALL OVER THE W

The 1st hair clipper in the U.S. was patented and manufactured by George Henry Coates in 1876. The clipper was considered superior to those in Europe. Coates made 100 different styles of clippers for humans and animals and mailed 12,000,000 clipper parts throughout the world. His factory at 227 Chandler St. had one full acre of floor space.

The 1st to develop the wind chill factor was Dr. Paul Siple, a leading American Antarctic explorer and geographer, who received his PhD from Clark University in 1939. The wind chill factor measures the combined effects of temperature and wind velocity on the loss of heat from human skin. While in Antarctica, Dr. Siple named a range the "Clark Mountains" and named its five peaks after his geography professors. His coined phrase, "wind chill factor," now dominates winter weather reports.

The First in
INVENTIONS
in the U.S.A.

The 1st monkey wrench

in the U.S. was invented in 1840 by brothers Loring Coes and Aury Gates Coes at the Northworks building on Grove St. It is rumored that it was given the name "monkey wrench" because it could be used with one hand, while holding a banana in the other!

The 1st power reel and intermediate twist guides,

which provided the necessary quarter turn for metal manufacturing, were invented by Charles H. Morgan. He was notable for the continuous rolling mill known the world over as the Morgan Mill. The Morgan Construction Company, located at 15 Belmont St., was formed in 1891. It is now part of Siemens Industry.

The first piano wire manufactured

in the U.S. was made by Ichabod Washburn, in 1850. He was nine years old when he started working. He was a philanthropist, as well as a master at wire manufacturing, and he gifted The Washburn Shops, which became a part of WPI.

One of the 1st street sprinklers

in the U.S. was invented in 1895 by Worcester's George T. Aitchison. It must have been entertaining for children to watch the driver on a horse-cart push a lever that sprinkled a width of 25 feet of water onto the street.

The 1st successful hydraulic direct-action plunger elevator

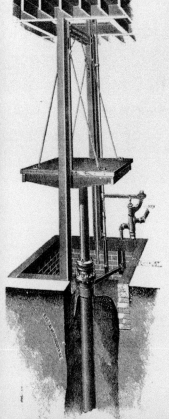

was made in Worcester at the Washburn Shops at WPI in 1868. Charles H. Morgan designed the elevator and Milton P. Higgins made the drawings. The elevator was so successful that it went from a one-story lift to a passenger elevator. Otis Elevator, still in business today, bought into these beginnings.

The 1st inventor and sole manufacturer of the Brownell Twister,

which made hard and soft twine, was George Loomis Brownell, in 1895. He opened shops on Union St. with one style of machine. He later was awarded U.S. and foreign patents for all his varieties of machines for spinning and twisting cotton, flax, hemp, silk, jute, wire and paper. Brownell lived on John St. in Worcester.

The First People in the U.S.A.

was held in downtown Worcester on October 23-24, 1850, at Main Street's Brinley Hall, where a plaque at 340 Main St. is today. More than 1,000 men and women from eleven different states demanded women's right to vote, to own property, and to be admitted to higher education. It would take another 70 years for women to win the right to vote. Worcester activist and abolitionist Abby Kelley Foster was a keynote speaker.

The 1st female member of the U.S. Cabinet

was Frances Perkins, who was appointed Secretary of Labor by President Franklin Delano Roosevelt in 1933. She served for eleven years and pioneered New Deal legislation that created Social Security and laws to protect workers' rights. She attended Classical High School in Worcester, and the Frances Perkins Branch Library, located at 470 West Boylston St., is named for her.

The 1st woman executed

in the U.S. under the American judicial system was Bathsheba Spooner, at the age of 32. On July 2, 1778, a pregnant Spooner and the soldiers she had hired to kill her husband were hanged before a crowd of 5,000 spectators in what is known today as Worcester's Washington Square.

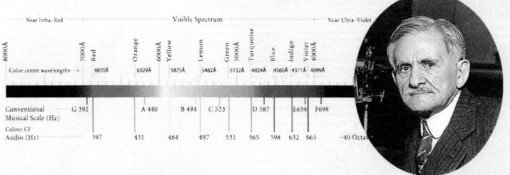

Abby Kelley Foster

The first American scientist to win a Nobel Prize

was Dr. Albert A. Michelson, a physics professor at Clark University. In 1907, Michelson's work measuring the number of wave lengths of the red light of cadmium contained in a meter won him this prestigious award. This discovery made it possible to standardize the meter and contributed to finding a set measurement for the speed of light.

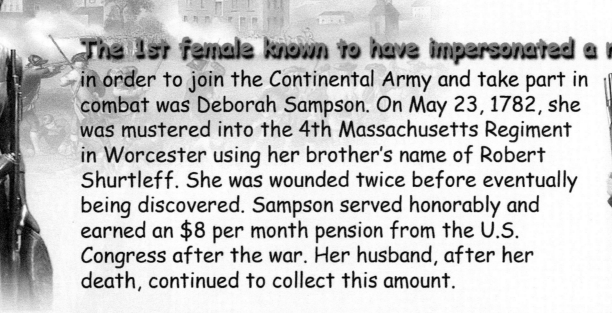

The 1st female known to have impersonated a man

in order to join the Continental Army and take part in combat was Deborah Sampson. On May 23, 1782, she was mustered into the 4th Massachusetts Regiment in Worcester using her brother's name of Robert Shurtleff. She was wounded twice before eventually being discovered. Sampson served honorably and earned an $8 per month pension from the U.S. Congress after the war. Her husband, after her death, continued to collect this amount.

The First People
in the U.S.A.

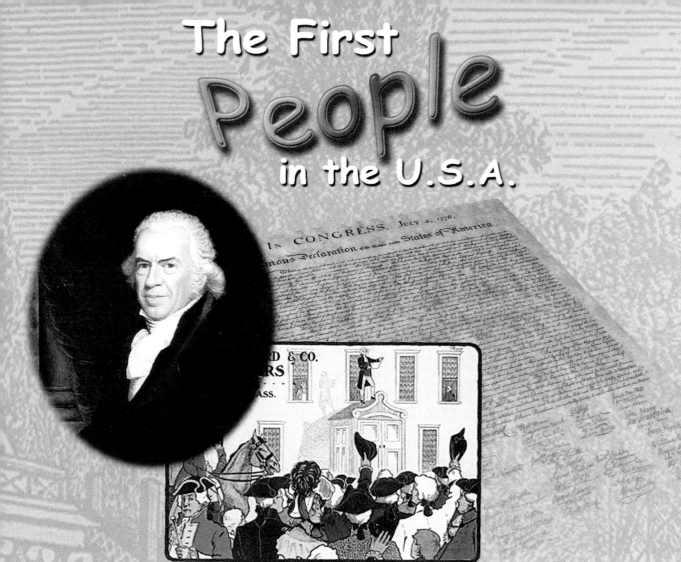

The 1st public reading of the Declaration of Independence
of the United States was performed in Worcester by Isaiah Thomas in 1776. A marker stands in front of Worcester City Hall where he flagged down the horse and rider carrying the Declaration down Main St. toward Boston. Thomas was the 1st to publish the Declaration in his newspaper, the *Massachusetts Spy*.

The 1st true field guide for bird watchers

printed in color was Chester A. Reed's famous Bird Guide: Land Birds East of the Rockies, published in 1906, and his western version, published in 1913. Reed was a devout, dedicated student of birdlife, though he graduated from WPI as an electrical engineer. All his life, he observed, sketched and photographed birds in their natural habitats. He wanted his field guide to be in color so other Americans could identify the birds more easily. Reed died at age 36 and is buried at Hope Cemetery.

The 1st history of the United States

was written over a period of 50 years by George Bancroft. He was a diplomat and U.S. Secretary of the Navy, and he founded the U.S. Naval Academy at Annapolis in 1845. Congress asked Bancroft to give the eulogy at President Abraham Lincoln's funeral. Bancroft School and Bancroft Hotel are among the many things in Worcester named for him; Bancroft Tower was built in his memory. A marker on Salisbury St. celebrates Bancroft's birthplace.

The First
Places
in the U.S.A.

The 1st Armenian church

in this country, Holy Saviour, was built in Worcester in 1890. It was constructed on Laurel St., under the charge of Father Hovsep Sarajian, from Constantinople, Turkey. In 1952, a new church was consecrated for their congregation, and they now worship at the Armenian Church of Our Saviour, located at 87 Salisbury St. The Laurel St. building still stands.

Among the 1st public land purchased

by a community for the purpose of a public park was Elm Park. The City of Worcester purchased 27 acres on March 15, 1854, as the New Common. The landscape was designed by E.W. Lincoln, based on the principles of Frederick Law Olmsted, who designed Central Park. In 1910, Olmsted and his brother were hired to review the plans for Elm Park and modify certain areas. The full loop of sidewalk encircling the park measures three-quarters of a mile.

The 1st pastoral training practice

focusing on compassionate treatment of the mentally ill was started at Worcester State Hospital by Reverend Dr. Anton Boisen and his colleagues in 1925. It is still the preeminent model for the clinical training of theological students.

The 1st building

in the nation to be constructed with an all-glass-and-steel exterior is Higgins Armory. It was designed for John Higgins, owner of Worcester Pressed Steel Company, to house his collection of armor. Higgins Armory opened its doors on January 12, 1931.

The 1st national historical association

in the country was the American Antiquarian Society, founded in 1812 by Isaiah Thomas. He wanted to "encourage the collection and preservation of the Antiquities of our country, and of precious and valuable production in Art and nature [that] have a tendency to enlarge the sphere." As founder of the largest publishing house in America, Thomas printed the 1st dictionary in 1788 and Bible in 1791. Isaiah would be happy to know his printing press has found the perfect home at 185 Salisbury St.

The 1st museum

to acquire a painting from French Impressionist Claude Monet's "Water Lilies" series was Worcester Art Museum. The oil painting was completed in 1908 and purchased by the museum in 1910.

The First in Space in the U.S.A.

The 1st book on the moon

was entitled *Robert Hutchings Goddard: Father of the Space Age.* The book was flown on Apollo 11 for America's first moon landing on July 20, 1969. Astronaut Edwin "Buzz" Aldrin, Jr. dated the leather-bound book and presented it to Esther Goddard, who left it to Clark's Goddard Library.

The 1st rocket

apparatuses were patented in 1914 by Dr. Robert Goddard, a professor at Clark University and member of WPI's class of 1908. He launched the 1st liquid-fueled rocket in America in 1926. Space travel started right here in Worcester.

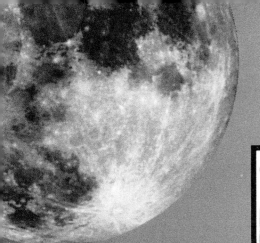

The 1st anti-G suits

and valves used by pilots of tactical fighter aircraft were designed to prevent pilots from blacking out when pulling out of high-speed dives. This photo shows one of many prototypes designed and built by David M. Clark. The suits have been worn, from World War II to the present day, by pilots of high-performance aircraft.

The 1st to speak from the moon

to the earth was astronaut Neil Armstrong. What made this feat possible? The communication cap (known as a "Snoopy cap") produced by David Clark Company, located at 360 Franklin St. This equipment allowed Neil Armstrong to speak his famous words from the moon to the earth: "That's one small step for man, one giant leap for mankind."

The 1st U.S. space walk

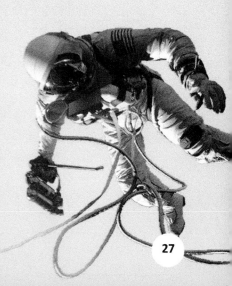

was completed in June, 1965 by astronaut Edward Higgins White, II. Worcester's David Clark Company manufactured all of NASA's Gemini space suits, including the suit worn by White. Since 1941, David Clark Company has built suits for NASA and the United States Air Force for all of their high-altitude programs. Famous pilots who have worn the suits include Chuck Yeager, John Glenn and Neil Armstrong.

The First in
SPORTS
in the U.S.A.

The 1st perfect game

in Major League Baseball was pitched in Worcester by J. Lee Richmond on June 12, 1880. The game pitted Richmond's Worcesters against the Cleveland Blues. After he retired, Richmond became a physician and a professor. Becker College, at 61 Sever St., has erected a monument to Richmond in their courtyard, where the game was originally played (then the Worcester Agricultural Fairgrounds).

The 1st 100-mile bicycle road race

took place between Worcester and Boston on October 6, 1883, and was sponsored by the Boston Bicycle Club. Thomas Midgely of Worcester won in 9 hours, 47 minutes. The second-place finisher clocked in at 10 hours, 44 minutes.

The 1st candlepin bowling

establishment was opened on Pearl St. in 1880 by Justin White. He designed the 12-inch-high pin we know today. White was given the title "1st Champion Candlepin Bowler" for reaching a score of 133.

Baseball's 1st curveball pitch

was a strike thrown in Worcester in 1867 by W.A. "Candy" Cummings, a pitcher for the Brooklyn Stars. He originally got his idea from tossing clamshells on the beach and finally perfected his technique into a curveball. The Baseball Hall of Fame recognizes Cummings for transforming the sport into a science.

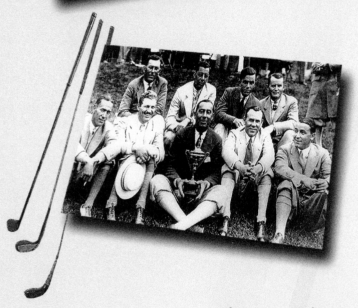

The 1st Ryder Cup

international golf competition was held in 1927 at Worcester Country Club, located at 2 Rice St. In this first contest, the U.S. team, captained by Walter Hagen, handily defeated the team from Great Britain, 9.5 to 2.5.

The 1st black American bicyclist

to set seven world records was Marshall "Major" Taylor. His career began in 1892 and ended in 1910. Despite facing extreme prejudice, he became known as the fastest bicyclist in the world. He lived on Hobson Ave. and has a street named for him—Major Taylor Boulevard. At the entrance to the Worcester Public Library is a sculptured monument of the "Worcester Whirlwind."

The First in the U.S.A.

Believe It or Not

Substantial Money Awards to be Given the Schoolboys and Girls Who Kill the Most Flies Before July 1

THE RACE IS NOW ON. FURTHER DETAILS WILL BE ANNOUNCED FROM DAY TO DAY

Dr. Hodge's perfected fly trap, with which he exterminated the housefly in the vicinity of his May St. home.

16,267,088 DEAD FLIES!

This is the "catch" at Worcester, Massachusetts, last summer—forty bushels of vanquished enemies of public comfort and health. As spoils of war, we have a heap of garden fertilizer

Fly Killing Will Begin Thursday at 6 P. M. and Continue Until 8 P. M. July 13, and The Telegram Will Pay $550 to Those Who Bring In the Most Dead Ones

Got any flies? The Only is going to take them all, and pay cash for them! The Only will take them all, in either grill or car load lots, except it won't take them on the hoof. They must be dead flies, and must, otherwise conform to the conditions named in the formal offer below; nearly without a fly!

It is to be the first city in the world to attempt to drive forth the white man's pest which carries germs of disease to the home and to the person. The Only has printed articles set-forth the views in detail of Prof. Hodge of Clark Uni-versity, explaining the danger of the house fly and how a city may exterminate it.

For several weeks

The Right Plan of Campaign for the War on the Fly
on the Farm and in the City

HOW THE EXTERMINATON OF THE TYPHOID OR FILTH-DISEASE PESTS SHOULD BE CARRIED ON "RIGHT SIDE UP"

By C. F. HODGE

THE PLAN to exterminate the typhoid, or filth-disease fly published in LA FOLLETTE'S last spring (April 15) has had a season in which to make good. That it has done so wherever it has been at all possible to apply it has been practically demonstrated. So far as flies are concerned, in case of the isolated home, it has done away with the need of screen windows and doors, and it has made possible the enjoy-ment of meals on unscreened porches without a fly to annoy—a veritable release from our summer fly screen prison bars.

The plan as published insisted on beginning early. A pair in April or May means millions in August. So simple—operation in mid-summer, with a land farm and country

Dr. Clifton Hodge of Clark University, who studied the life of the housefly, waged war on the fly in Worcester. The city was to be without a fly—well, nearly without a fly! Worcester was to be the first city in the world to drive away this pest that carried disease into the home.

A city-wide campaign was launched in June 1911, offering prizes to the schoolchildren who could kill the most flies. Substantial monetary prizes, donated by public-spirited citizens, were offered, and enough money was pledged to assure the plan's success.

The contest rules stipulated that children could "catch the flies in traps or insect nets, and they must kill them—in scalding water or over a gas flame—and spread them out in the sun and dry them thoroughly and put them in a clean paper bag. All lots that are wet or lots in which the flies are mixed with dirt or sand or any other foreign matter will be thrown out of the competition entirely."

Dr. Hodge tested his own fly trap on top of the garbage can at his home on May St. In a remarkably short time, there was not a single fly to be found at his home. He had absolutely proved with this test that the fly could be exterminated.

Nice job, Dr. Hodge. Do you think this is why Worcester is nicknamed Wormtown???

Just to get you started, here are three examples of the clues and questions you will find in the next section.

Do you know?

1. During the mid-to-late nineteenth century, E. W. Vaill patented and manufactured over one hundred different styles of his popular chairs in Worcester.
Do you know what kind of chair he manufactured?

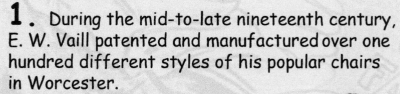

2. Less than a week after Fenway Park opened on April 26, 1912, a baseball player hit the ballpark's first home run. The homer cleared the 31-foot-high left field fence. This baseball player lived at 43 Austin St. in Worcester and is buried at St. John's Cemetery.
Do you know this player's name?

3. Robert Benchley, born in Worcester in 1889, was a pioneering humorist, as well as an actor, filmmaker and critic. His son, Nathaniel, wrote a biography of his father, and his grandson, Peter, is best known as the author of a famous novel and also co-wrote the screenplay of its Oscar-nominated film adaptation.
Do you know the name of Peter Benchley's book and film?

Now you're on your own!

Answers: 1. Folding Chair / 2. Hugh Bradley / 3. *Jaws*

DO YOU KNOW...?

50 Questions and Answers

👉 **More interesting Facts & Tidbits!**

👉 **Helpful hints are found across each two-page spread!**

FACTS ABOUT WORCESTER

Do you know?

1. Esther Forbes was a children's author and the first female member of the American Antiquarian Society. In 1943, she won the Newbery Medal for her book about a silversmith's apprentice at the time of the Revolution.
Do you know the title of this book?

2. Ted Williams, the Red Sox slugger, hit his first professional home run in Worcester in 1939.
Do you know on what field the game was played?

3. The Worcester Music Festival was inaugurated in 1858 and is the oldest ongoing music festival in the nation. It was originally presented by the Worcester County Music Association.
Do you know this group's name today?

4. Coney Island on Southbridge St. is famous for its delicious hot dogs. There used to be a famous hot dog stand on Lake Ave., near Lake Quinsigamond. The new owners have relocated to 340 Main St.
Do you know what this hot dog stand is called?

Match the questions with the helpful hints.

5. She grew up in Worcester and opened a school at age 14, headed the Union army nurses during the Civil War, and advocated for compassionate treatment of the mentally ill.
Do you know her name?

6. Michael Orland began his musical career on Kenilworth Rd. in Worcester. After he went to see *Mary Poppins* a few times with his family, he sat down at the piano and played the songs by ear. He is now an acclaimed musical director.
Do you know the music-based TV show he has been with since the beginning?

7. In 1908, this Worcester company employed 1,200 women, making it the largest employer of women in the U.S. at that time. It had progressive working conditions and benefits.
Do you know the name of the company?

8. He was a graduate of Worcester Academy who co-founded the Youth International ("Yippie") Party and stood trial as one of the Chicago Seven.
Do you know who this radical of the '60s and '70s was?

Keep guessing!

9. This poet was born in 1905 and wrote poems about his boyhood in Worcester. He won the Pulitzer Prize for *Selected Poems, 1928-1958* and in 2000 was named the United States Poet Laureate.
Do you know this poet's name?

10. He grew up on Worcester's south side, graduated from St. Peter's Central Catholic High School and began his entertainment career as a stand-up comedian. In response to the December 1999 Worcester Cold Storage Warehouse fire, in which six Worcester firefighters died, he established a foundation to support firehouses.
Do you know who this generous actor and comedian is?

11. Albina Osipowich, a graduate of North High School, was 17 years old when she won double gold medals at the 1928 Amsterdam Olympics.
Do you know in what sport she competed?

12. On October 1, 2011, she was honored and inducted into the National Women's Hall of Fame in Seneca Falls, NY. On October 22, 2011, she was also inducted into the Abolition Hall of Fame and Museum in Peterboro, NY.
Do you know who this abolitionist and Worcester resident was?

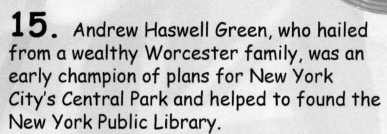

13. Edward Davis Jones was born in the rectory of the Pleasant Street Baptist Church, where his father was a minister. He was a graduate of Worcester Academy and from an early age was known as someone who could read and understand financial reports better than anyone else.
Do you know which two companies he co-founded?

14. This famous songwriter attended Worcester Academy and said his talent for writing songs started in Worcester. He wrote the famous songs "Night and Day," "I've Got You Under My Skin," and "Anything Goes."
Do you know the name of this composer?

15. Andrew Haswell Green, who hailed from a wealthy Worcester family, was an early champion of plans for New York City's Central Park and helped to found the New York Public Library.
Do you know what park, located atop a 777-foot hill, is named for his family?

16. This anarchist was deported back to Russia after being imprisoned for hindering WWI conscription in 1917 and ran an ice cream parlor in the city (thought to be on Providence St., Winter St. or Main St.).
Do you know her name?

Awesome!

17. John "Jack" Smith was born and grew up in Worcester. In 1956, he graduated from St. John's High School in Shrewsbury. He eventually became president and CEO of one of the largest American automotive corporations.
Do you know which company he led?

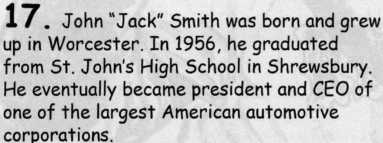

18. Samuel Winslow, once mayor of Worcester, was the largest manufacturer in the world of a particular sport product.
Do you know what he manufactured?

WORCESTER
State University

19. Craig C. Mello, PhD, of the University of Massachusetts Medical School in Worcester, was honored with a prestigious award in 2006 for the discovery of RNA interference.
Do you know what award he received?

20. Nicholas Gage is famous for his two autobiographical memoirs, *Eleni* and *A Place for Us*, which describe his escape from his family's communist-occupied village and his immigrant experience in Worcester.
Do you know from which country he escaped?

21. Noteworthy performers at this venue include: Mark Twain, Charles Dickens, Henry David Thoreau, John Philip Sousa, and presidents Theodore Roosevelt, William Howard Taft and Woodrow Wilson.
Do you know where they spoke?

22. This church's choirs are the oldest of their type still functioning in the U.S. The men and boys choir has sung continuously since 1868, and the women and girls choir, later to be called the St. Cecilia Choir, has been singing continuously since 1897.
Do you know the name of this church?

23. The first Massachusetts teaching college to have a chapter of Kappa Delta Pi, the international education honor society, is a Worcester university.
Do you know which one?

24. In 1891, Clinton Marshall developed a machine at the Washburn & Moen Co. in Worcester. He ended up heading American Steel & Wire in the city.
Do you know what he worked all his life manufacturing?

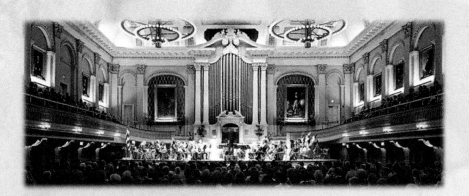

Don't give up!

25. She was a prize-winning poet who was born in Worcester and lived from 1911-1979. She won a 1956 Pulitzer Prize for *Poems: North & South/A Cold Spring.*
Do you know this poet's name?

26. Rich Gedman lived on Lafayette St., attended St. Peter-Marian High School and played in the 1986 World Series.
Do you know the name of his baseball team?

27. Actress Alisan Porter starred with James Belushi in the 1991 Hollywood film *Curly Sue.* She and her mother, Laura Klein, both taught at the Charlotte Klein Dance Center in Worcester. Both women also performed in the same Broadway musical, and even played the same role, exactly 30 years apart.
Do you know what musical it was?

28. This early U.S. President came to Worcester to teach school after graduating from Harvard College in 1755.
Do you know which President?

31. He was a "Tin Pan Alley" songwriter, raised in a three-decker at 79 Harrison St. With two of his brothers, he wrote "The Old Lamplighter" about his Worcester days. Other songs include "Don't Sit Under the Apple Tree (With Anyone Else but Me)" and "Rose O'Day." He wrote over 60 songs, many sung by Bing Crosby, Nat King Cole and Ella Fitzgerald.
Do you know his name?

29. Meredith Vieira got her start in broadcasting as the afternoon drive newscaster at WORC radio station.
Do you know the game show she is famous for hosting?

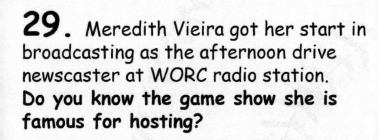

32. Olive Higgins Prouty, born and raised in Worcester, wrote a novel about a mother rejected by her socialite daughter that was first made into a play, then a silent movie, later a movie with Barbara Stanwyck, and finally adapted again with Bette Midler.
Do you know what she titled the book?

30. Samuel N. Behrman (1893-1973), author and screenwriter, wrote a book of nostalgic and comic sketches about growing up in Worcester's Jewish community. In 1958, this book was made into a Broadway play starring Maureen Stapleton, Eli Wallach and Clifford Davis.
Do you know the name of his book?

33. The oldest operating hardware store in the nation is located at 156 Main St. It opened in 1782 and still specializes in hard-to-find items in an easy-to-find store.
Do you know the name of this hardware store?

35. Worcester's Jesse Burkett Little League All-Stars were the first team from Central Massachusetts to qualify for the Little League World Series (August 2002, in Japan). **Do you know what their namesake Hall of Famer's batting specialty was?**

36. The largest theater organ in New England is located at The Hanover Theatre for the Performing Arts, ranked one of the top 100 theaters in the world. They hold events throughout the year to listen to this fabulous organ.
Do you know its name?

34. This 14-term congressman, who served from 1947-1974, was on the House Judiciary Committee that conducted the Watergate hearings. He offered the resolution to impeach President Richard M. Nixon in 1974.
Do you know his name?

39. Arthur Kennedy was a Broadway and Hollywood actor and the son of a Worcester dentist. He received five Oscar nominations and starred in *High Sierra, Peyton Place,* and *Lawrence of Arabia.* He also won a Tony in 1949 for his role as Willy Loman's son, Biff, in an Arthur Miller play.
Do you know the name of this Tony Award-winning play?

37. Bob Cousy and Tom Heinsohn are both Hall of Famers for the Boston Celtics and played for the same college team.
Do you know which Worcester college they attended?

38. St. Pierre Manufacturing of Worcester, located on E. Mountain St., in 1946 received the coveted U.S. Navy "E" award for excellence for producing 27 million pounds of anchor chain for WWII. They are the largest manufacturer of equipment for a sport played both professionally and in the backyard.
Do you know the name of this sport?

40. This 52-stop, 3,504-pipe instrument is the oldest unrelocated and unaltered four-keyboard organ in the western hemisphere. Built in 1864, it's located at Mechanics Hall and has been featured in the major motion picture *The Bostonians.*
Do you know the name of this organ?

41. Denholm's, built in 1881, upscaled their department store in 1964 by renovating and adding escalators. The first-to-third floor escalators were exquisite, with rococo-style decoration placed protectively between two panels of glass. The Denholm's escalators, located at 500 Main St., were the first of their kind to be installed in New England.
Do you know the name of these escalators?

43. After being released from a Texas prison, he worked in Worcester for about two weeks before returning south to his sweetheart Bonnie. They became an infamous bank-robbing duo.
Do you know his name?

42. Worcester Lunch Car Company produced almost 600 diners between 1906 and 1957. One of these diners still exists in its original location, across the street from the former factory.
Do you know the name of this diner?

44. There was a surprise 1981 concert by The Rolling Stones at Sir Morgan's Cove on Green Street. To this day, it is still considered a major event in the city of Worcester.
Do you know the name of the club today?

46. He is a former *Telegram & Gazette* editorial cartoonist who created the original "Pat Patriot" football logo. His cartoon featuring a Red Sox slugger from one of his sports columns is on this page.
Do you know this cartoonist's name?

45. He was a famous author, statesman, scientist, musician, inventor and printer who, on a visit to Worcester, helped fix the press of Isaiah Thomas at the *Massachusetts Spy.*
Do you know who this famous patriot was?

Good job!
Buen trabajo!

47. Michael McGrath, a native of Worcester, graduated from St. Peter's Central Catholic High School. He received the 2012 Tony Award for the best featured actor in a musical for playing a wisecracking mobster, and he thanked his family in Worcester during his acceptance speech.
Do you know the name of this Broadway musical?

48. The construction of three-deckers was popular during the late 1800s through the 1930s because it provided inexpensive housing for the waves of immigrants arriving to work in Worcester factories. There are eight distinctive styles of three-decker, distinguished by decade and neighborhood. In 1990 many of these buildings were listed on the National Register of Historic Places.
Do you know how many three-deckers remain in Worcester today?

49. M.J. Whittall built a mill on Southbridge St. in Worcester for the manufacture of fine woven Oriental rugs and carpets. If you own one today, it's a Worcester treasure.
Do you know what company has taken over the building?

50. One eye is larger than the other, the mouth is not a perfect arc, and the ends are arched (i.e., not straight lines).
Do you know what we are talking about?

Did you have fun?

Answers begin on page 76.

Acknowledgments...

- **Thank you** to ⌣⌣⌣ⵔⵔⵔ [worcester arts council] for the 2011 Grant. It is better to be right than rushed. Thank you for your patience.

- **Thank you** to Memorial Foundation for the Blind for sponsoring a version of this book in braille, Talking Books and print.

- **Thank you** to Steven Rotman for your enthusiastic loyalty to Worcester and your contributions to the publication of this book.

- **Thank you** to Worcester Historical Museum, especially William D. Wallace, Executive Director, for sharing your knowledge of Worcester with humor and wit. Also, for all your assistance, many thanks to Museum librarian Robyn Christensen and your staff.

- **Thank you** to Worcester Public Library: Mark Contois, Head Librarian; Anne S. Hrobsky, Youth Division. Also, Doreen Velnich, Head of Reference Division and Branches, Joy Hennig, Local History Librarian, and Jim Izatt, Director of Talking Book Library.

- **Thank you** for all your hard work to Clark University research interns Christine Mullaney, KC Cutrona and bibliographer Kathryn L. Natale. Also, intern Rachael Fahlstrom of Bancroft School's volunteer program.

- **Consultants:** William D. Wallace, Executive Director, Worcester Historical Museum; Thomas Doughton, Professor, College of the Holy Cross; John Anderson, Professor Emeritus, College of the Holy Cross; Albert B. Southwick, Retired Chief Editorial Writer, Telegram & Gazette; Ashley Cataldo, Assistant Librarian, American Antiquarian Society; Deborah Packard, Executive Director, Preservation Worcester; Susan McDaniel Ceccacci, Education Director, Preservation Worcester; Nancy Avila, Executive Assistant, Worcester Women's History Project; Fordyce Williams, Coordinator of Archives and Special Collections, Clark University; Jane Salerno, Clark University Marketing Consultant; Margaret Anderson, Library Archivist at the George C. Gordon Library at WPI; Jim Wolken, Office of Marketing & Communications, WPI; Ellen More, Jeffrey Geller, and Kristine Reinhard, The Lamar Soutter Library, University of Massachusetts Medical School.

- **Text and Graphics Contributors:** All Saints Church, American Antiquarian Society, Becker College, College of the Holy Cross, David Clark Company, Elwood Adams Hardware, Hanover Theatre, Higgins Armory, MA Audubon/Broad Meadow Brook, Mechanics Hall, Music Worcester, Inc., St. Pierre Manufacturing Corp., Worcester Academy, Worcester Art Museum, Worcester Country Club, Worcester Historical Museum, Worcester Parks & Recreation, Worcester State University, Worcester Telegram & Gazette, Worcester Department of Economic Development and Neighborhoods, and Worcester Polytechnic Institute.

Also, Phil Bissell, cartoonist; Donald Featherstone, sculptor; June Benoit, photographer; Dave O'Gara, retired Worcester DJ; Charles Ball, Connie Tuttle, Eve Rifkah and Janet Sarwood.

Appreciation...

- **My deep appreciation to Erica and Wyatt Wade** of Davis Publications, for starting me out in the right direction.
- **Tom Campbell** of King Printing in Lowell for bringing the book to an end and a new beginning.
- **Cheryl Cory**, editor and author of *Must've Done Something Good*. You sure did when you took on the job of editing this book.
- **JeanPaul Raymond**, graphic designer, who brought Worcester into the limelight with his artistic touch and creative graphics.
- **Robin Wrighton**, book designer, who took us from page to page and brought this book creatively together.
- **Liz Steele**, publisher at Lakshmi Books, who was excited to see a new book about Worcester's history. As a former teacher, she could see students enjoying entertaining and educational presentations. She's a believer.

Special Thanks...

Special Thanks to all my family for their patience and help that I will never take for granted. My sisters, Pricilla who never said no to research and June who volunteered her professional photography. Thank you to all who answered the call for help and contributed in any way to this book. You know who you are – you've given back to the City of Worcester, and I truly appreciate it.

You Never Know When There Will Be Another First For Worcester!

High altitude balloon pilot's jump suit marks another FIRST for Worcester's David Clark Company.

A team of about 50 people worked for four years on his state-of-the-art pressure suit for a stunning feat that will be studied to determine how U.S. military pilots, astronauts, and even passengers aboard future commercial space flights might be able to survive similarly high falls.

Pilot Felix Baumgartner and technical project director Art Thompson celebrate after the successful jump in Roswell, N.M.
(THE ASSOCIATED PRESS/RED BULL STRATOS)

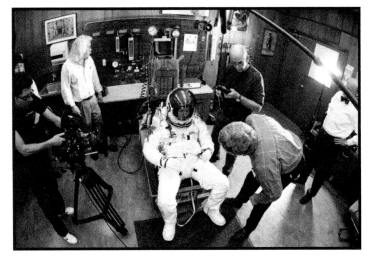

Felix Baumgartner made a record-breaking jump in a suit designed by the Worcester firm David Clark Company, which has been pioneering air and space crew protective gear since 1941.
(David Clark Company/Red Bull Stratos)

"Fearless Felix" Baumgartner, WORLD RECORD HOLDER!

On October 14, 2012, Felix Baumgartner jumped from 128,100 feet. That's over 24 miles above the Earth's surface! He reached a record-breaking speed of 833.9 miles per hour, becoming the first man to break the speed of sound in a freefall from the stratosphere. Wearing only a David Clark Company pressure suit, Felix became the first man to fly at supersonic speed without an airplane.

Do you know a **FIRST IN THE U.S.A.** that happened in Worcester,
or an interesting fact about Worcester you didn't see in this book?

If so, send your ideas in with your name, contact info, and source and we'll add it to our online version of

Worcester Stacks Up!

WORCESTER FIRSTS	WORCESTER FUN FACTS

SEND YOUR WORCESTER FIRSTS OR FUN FACTS TO: info@worcesterstacksup.com or visit www.worcesterstacksup.com
Mail to: Lakshmi Books, P.O. Box 1205, Leominster, MA 01453

FOR THOSE WHO WANT TO KNOW MORE

Do you want to know **more?**

Now that you have learned so much about Worcester, you can use the following bibliography to write a report for school, research a project, or write your own book!

BIBLIOGRAPHY

FIRST IN THE U.S.A. • Arts

The Beatles **10**

O'Gara, Dave. "Re: The Beatles & Meredith Vieira." Message to the author. 8 Apr. 2012. E-mail.

Spizer, Bruce. *The Beatles Swan Song: "She Loves You" & Other Records.* New Orleans, LA: 498 Productions, 2007. Print.

"Casey at the Bat" **11**

Abramoff, Larry, Gloria Abramoff, and Ann Lindblad. *Favorite Places of Worcester County: A Guide to Shopping, Dining, Recreation, Sightseeing, History, Facts & Fun in Central Massachusetts.* Worcester, MA: Chandler House, 1999. Print.

Zezima, Katie. "In 'Casey' Rhubarb, 2 Cities Cry 'Foul!'." NYTimes.com. The New York Times Company, 31 Mar. 2004. Web.

"The Lion Sleeps Tonight" **11**

Hornby, Nick, and Ben Schafer. *Da Capo Best Music Writing 2001: The Year's Finest Writing on Rock, Pop, Jazz, Country & More.* New York: Da Capo Press, 2001. Print.

Malan, Rian. "In the Jungle." *Rolling Stone*: 25 May 2000. Print.

O'Gara, Dave. "Re: The Beatles & Meredith Vieira." Message to the author. 8 Apr. 2012. E-mail.

Pink Flamingo **10**

Featherstone, Don. "Pink Flamingo Origins." Telephone interview. Mar. 2012.

Luttrell, Martin. "Pink Flamingo Fading to Black." Telegram.com. Worcester Telegram & Gazette Corp., 22 Sept. 2006. Web.

Owen, Paula J. "Fitchburg's Featherstone Goes Hollywood." <u>Telegram.com</u>. Worcester Telegram & Gazette Corp., 18 Feb. 2011. Web.

Welu, Jim. "Re: Pink Flamingo." Message to the author. 5 Mar. 2012. E-mail.

Honan, William H. "H. R. Ball, 79, Ad Executive Credited With Smiley Face." <u>NYTimes.com</u>. New York Times Company, 14 Apr. 2001. Web.

"Introduction to Smiley Licensing & Merchandising." <u>Worldsmile.org</u>. Harvey Ball World Smile Foundation. Web.

Loughlin, Jeff. "He Was Such a Nice Guy." *Worcester Magazine*: 27 Oct. 2005: 11. Print.

History. "Valentine's Day." <u>History.com</u>. A&E Television Networks, LLC. Web.

Southwick, Albert B. "Valentine's Mistress Apparently Spent Life Unattached." *Telegram & Gazette* [Worcester, MA]. Print.

GRAPHICS CREDITS - FIRST IN THE U.S.A. • Arts

Beatles Gold Record Cufflinks. 2006. Photograph. <u>Clevercufflinks.com</u>. Clever Products Corporation, June 2006. Web.

Izzat, Jim. Casey at the Bat Letter. Photograph. Worcester Public Library, Worcester, MA.

Raymond, JeanPaul. Casey at the Bat. 2012.

Benoit, June. Photograph. Flamingo. 2012.

Donated Sample. Cado Manufacturing, Fitchburg, MA. 2012.

Graphic. Worcester Historical Museum, Worcester, MA.

Photograph. Worcester Historical Museum, Worcester, MA.

Graphic. Raymond, JeanPaul. Lion. 2012.

American Psychiatric Association **12**

Grob, Gerald N. *The State and the Mentally Ill: A History of Worcester State Hospital in Massachusetts, 1830-1920.*
  Chapel Hill: Univ. of North Carolina, 1966. Print.

More, Ellen S. "WSH." Message to the author. 9 Jan. 2012. E-mail.

American Psychological Association **12**

"About Clark: Historical Timeline." Clarku.edu. Clark University. Web.

"APA History and Archives." APA.org. American Psychological Association. Web.

Kane, Joseph Nathan. *Famous First Facts: A Record of First Happenings, Discoveries, and Inventions in American History.* 4th ed.
  New York: H.W. Wilson, 1981. Print.

Anthropology Doctorate **13**

Darnell, Regna. "The Emergence of Academic Anthropology at the University of Pennsylvania." Journal of the History of the
  Behavioral Sciences 6.1 (1970): 80-92. Onlinelibrary.wiley.com. John Wiley & Sons, Inc., 18 Apr. 2006. Web.

Williams, Fordyce. "Re: Final Proofing." Message to the author. 21 Nov. 2011. E-mail.

Geography School **13**

Kane, Joseph Nathan. *Famous First Facts: A Record of First Happenings, Discoveries, and Inventions in American History.* 4th ed.
  New York: H.W. Wilson, 1981. Print.

Williams, Fordyce. "Re: Final Proofing." Message to the author. 21 Nov. 2011. E-mail.

Graduate Degree at Clark **13**

"A History of Innovation." Clarku.edu. Clark University. Web.

Williams, Fordyce. "Re: Final Proofing." Message to the author. 21 Nov. 2011. E-mail.

Robotics Degree **13**

Anderson, Margaret F. "Re: Your Worcester Book of Firsts." Message to the author. 9 Apr. 2012. E-mail.

WPI Robotics Engineering Department. "WPI: First in Robotics Engineering." WPI.edu. Worcester Polytechnic Institute. Web.

Sigmund Freud's Lectures **12**

Clark University Archives. "The 1909 Conferences." <u>Clarku.edu</u>. Clark University, 2009. Web.

Clark University Archives. "The Sigmund Freud and Carl Jung Lectures at Clark University." <u>Clarku.edu</u>. Clark University. Web.

Women's Classical Institution **13**

Callahan, Frank. "Re: WA Notables." Message to the author. 13 Feb. 2012. E-mail.

Tulloch, Donald. *Worcester, City of Prosperity.* Worcester, MA: Commonwealth Press, 1914. Print.

Worcester Women's History Project Newsletter 1.12 (Summer 2001). <u>WWHP.org</u>. Worcester Women's History Project. Web.

Wright, Martha Burt, ed. History of the Oread Collegiate Institute. New Haven: Tuttle, Morehouse & Taylor Co., 1905. Print.

GRAPHICS CREDITS - FIRST IN THE U.S.A. • Education

American Psychiatric Association **12**

Samuel B. Woodward. Worcester Historical Museum, Worcester, MA.

American Psychological Association **12**

Gutekunst, Frederick. Granville Stanley Hall. 1910. Photograph. <u>Wikipedia.org</u>. Wikimedia Foundation, Inc. Web.

Brain. Bill Kerr, 17 Mar. 2012. Web. <u>Billkerr2.blogspot.com</u>. T. S. Eggleston, 16 Apr. 2012. Web. <u>Theegglestongroup.com</u>.

Anthropology Doctorate **13**

Physical Anthropology. <u>Uprightdoctor.wordpress.com</u>. <u>Wordpress.com</u>, 19 Aug. 2010. Web.

Geography School **13**

Geography Map. <u>Clipartheaven.com</u>. Web.

Graduate Degree at Clark **13**

Photograph. Clark University, Worcester, MA.

Robotics Degree **13**

Wolken, James. Emblem. Worcester Polytechnic Institute, Worcester, MA.

Raymond, JeanPaul. Robot. 2012.

FIRST IN THE U.S.A. • Food

GRAPHICS CREDITS - FIRST IN THE U.S.A. • Food

FIRST IN THE U.S.A. • Health

Bacteriological Laboratory **15**

Kush, Bronislaus B. "Seven Structures Are Endangered." *Telegram & Gazette* [Worcester, MA]: 23 May 2007: B1. Print.

Preservation Worcester. "Belmont Hospital Laboratory." *Preservation Worcester Newsletter*: 2008. Print.

Federally-Licensed AIDS Test **15**

O'Sullivan, Kevin. "FW." Message to the author. 26 Apr. 2012. E-mail.

Sullivan, John. "AIDS Test." Message to the author. 13 Mar. 2012. E-mail.

Oral Contraceptive Pill **15**

"Dr. Pincus, Developer of Birth-Control Pill, Dies." *New York Times*: 23 Aug. 1967, Obituary sec. NYTimes.com. The New York Times Company. Web.

Nugent, Karen. "The Pill Turns 50." *Sunday Telegram* [Worcester, MA]: 23 May 2010. A1. Print.

"People & Events: Gregory Pincus (1903-1967)." PBS.org. Public Broadcasting Service, 2002. Web.

Sewage Disposal **15**

"Disposal of Sanitary Sewage." *Tracking Down the Roots of Our Sanitary Sewers.* Comp. Jon C. Schladweiler and Arizona Water Association. Sewerhistory.org. 15 Jan. 2002. Web.

Eddy, Harrison P. "Sewage Disposal at Worcester, Mass." *Journal of the American Chemical Society*: 16.10 (1894): 682-87. Print.

GRAPHICS CREDITS - FIRST IN THE U.S.A. • Health

Bacteriological Laboratory **15**

Photograph. Preservation Worcester, Worcester, MA.

Federally-Licensed AIDS Test **15**

P_Wei. AIDS Ribbon with Clipping Path. Istockphoto.com. iStockphoto LP. Web.

Oral Contraceptive Pill **15**

Raymond, JeanPaul. Pills. 2012.

Sewage Disposal **15**

Photograph. *Telegram & Gazette*, Worcester, MA. Print.

FIRST IN THE U.S.A. • Inventions

Brownell Twister **19**

    Nutt, Charles. *History of Worcester and its People.* Vol. 3. New York: Lewis Historical Publishing, 1919. Print.

Car Sprinkler **19**

    Aitchison, George T. Sprinkling-Wagon. Patent 549481. 12 Nov. 1895. Print.

    Biographical Review ... Containing Life Sketches of Leading Citizens of Worcester County, Massachusetts.
      Boston: Biographical Review Pub., 1899. Print.

    Sandrof, Ivan. "Aitchison Street." *Your Worcester Street.* Worcester, MA: Franklin Pub., 1948. Print.

Clipper **17**

    Lindvig, Astrid. "Worcester's Own Yankee Clipper." *Telegram & Gazette* [Worcester, MA]: 16 Sept. 1967. Print.

    Vaskas, Edmund J. "History Was Made Here." *Telegram & Gazette* [Worcester, MA]: 4 Aug. 1959. Print.

Envelope-Folding Machine **16**

    Pope, Nancy A. "Envelopes in the Machine Age." *EnRoute 6.2* (Spring 1997). Postalmuseum.si.edu. Smithsonian Institution. Web.

    Tulloch, Donald. *Worcester, City of Prosperity.* Worcester, MA: Commonwealth Press, 1914. Print.

Grinding Machine **17**

    Luttrell, Martin. "Ex-chief Praises Workers at Norton 125th." *Telegram & Gazette* [Worcester, MA]: 19 June 2010: A9. Print.

    "Norton: 125 Years in the Worcester Community." *Sunday Telegram* [Worcester, MA]: 20 June 2010: A5. Print.

    Tulloch, Donald. *Worcester, City of Prosperity.* Worcester, MA: Commonwealth Press, 1914. Print.

    WPI Mechanical Engineering. "The History of Washburn Shops." Me.wpi.edu. Worcester Polytechnic Institute, 6 Oct. 2006. Web.

Hydraulic Elevator **19**

    Higgins, Milton P. Improvement in Hydraulic Elevators. Patent 181263. 7 June 1876. Print.

    Tymeson, Mildred M. *Two Towers: The Story of Worcester Tech.* Worcester, MA: Worcester Polytechnic Institute, 1965. Print.

    WPI Mechanical Engineering. "The History of Washburn Shops." Me.wpi.edu. Worcester Polytechnic Institute, 6 Oct. 2006. Web.

Monkey Wrench **18**

    "Coes Wrench Co." Davistownmuseum.org. The Davistown Museum. Web.

"Death at Age of 94." *Worcester Daily Telegram*: 14 July 1906. Print.

Tulloch, Donald. *Worcester, City of Prosperity.* Worcester, MA: Commonwealth Press, 1914. Print.

Nutt, Charles. *History of Worcester and its People.* Vol. 3. New York: Lewis Historical Publishing, 1919. Print.

Tulloch, Donald. *Worcester, City of Prosperity.* Worcester, MA: Commonwealth Press, 1914. Print.

Rice, Franklin P. "Wire." *The Worcester of Eighteen Hundred and Ninety-eight: Fifty Years a City.*
   Worcester, MA: F.S. Blanchard, 1899. 457-460. Print.

George C. Gordon Library Archives. "Morgan Construction Collection." WPI.edu. Worcester Polytechnic Institute. Web.

Long, Tony. "Oct. 9, 1855: Music-Making a Steampunk Can Love." Wired.com. *Condé Nast*: 8 Oct. 2009. Web.

Roehl, Harvey N. "Harmony in Steam." Player Piano Treasury. New York: Vestal, 1961. MMDigest.com.
   Mechanical Music Digest: 7 June 1998. Web.

Crabtree, Jerome Bruce. *The Marvels of Modern Mechanism and Their Relation to Social Betterment.*
   Springfield, MA: King-Richardson, 1901. 612. Print.

Esposito, Andi. "'First American Typewriter Got Its Start Here." *Telegram & Gazette* [Worcester, MA]: 13 May 2011: A1. Print.

Sandrof, Ivan. "Worcester Man's Famed Early Typewriter Uncovered Recently in Cellar of Worcester Historical Society."
   Sunday Telegram [Worcester, MA]: 19 June 1960: 7-8. Print.

Clark University Advancement. "Clark-tic Research." Clarkconnect.clarku.edu. Clark University. Web.

Foley, Rich. "If It Feels Too Cold, Then Blame Paul Siple." Statelineobserver.com. *State Line Observer*: 30 Nov. 2011. Web.

Williams, Fordyce. "Re: Final Proofing." Message to the author. 21 Nov. 2011. E-mail.

GRAPHICS CREDITS - FIRST IN THE U.S.A. • Inventions

George L. Brownell. Photograph. Worcester Historical Museum, Worcester, MA.

FIRST IN THE U.S.A. • People

Bancroft, George **23**

Earle, Jr., Thomas. "Biography of a Historian." *Telegram & Gazette* [Worcester, MA]: 19 Sept. 1944. Print.

Hayward, Adrian. "Who Was George Bancroft?" *Worcester Daily Telegram*: 31 July 1958. Print.

Southwick, Albert B. "Great Historian George Bancroft Now Lost to History." *Sunday Telegram* [Worcester, MA]: 7 Oct. 2007: C3. Print.

Michelson, Albert A. **21**

"About Clark: Historical Timeline." Clarku.edu. Clark University. Web.

"Albert Abraham Michelson." *Selected Papers of Great American Physicists: The Bicentennial Commemorative Volume of The American Physical Society.* Ed. Spencer R. Weart. New York: American Institute of Physics, 1976. AIP.org. Web.

"History of Physics at Clark: The Michelson Era (1889 - 1892)." Clarku.edu. Clark University. Web.

"The Nobel Prize in Physics 1907." Nobelprize.org. Nobel Media AB. Web.

Williams, Fordyce. "Corrections." Message to the author. 3 Aug. 2011. E-mail.

Perkins, Frances **20**

"Frances Perkins Collection: Biographical Note." Asteria.fivecolleges.edu. Mount Holyoke College Archives and Special Collections. Web.

Reed, Chester A. **23**

Dunne, Pete. *Pete Dunne on Bird Watching: The How-to, Where-to, and When-to of Birding.* Boston: Houghton Mifflin, 2003. Print.

Green, Frances. "Worcester's Own Audubon." *Sunday Telegram* [Worcester, MA]: 31 July 1960: 21-22. Print.

Sampson, Deborah **21**

Bois, Danuta. "Deborah Sampson." Distinguishedwomen.com. *Women's Biographies: Distinguished Women of Past and Present.* 1998. Web.

Leonard, Patrick J. "Deborah Sampson: Official Heroine of the State of Massachusetts." Canton.org. Canton Massachusetts Historical Society, 16 Oct. 2006. Web.

Spooner, Bathsheba **20**

Jonswold, Miranda. "Trail of Bathsheba Spooner Is Re-enacted." *Telegram & Gazette* [Worcester, MA]: 5 June 2009: A1. Print.

Vaver, Anthony. "Early American Criminals: Bathsheba Spooner, Accessory to the Murder of Joshua Spooner; and James Buchanan, William Brooks, and Ezra Ross for Said Murder." Earlyamericancrime.com. 27 May 2009. Web.

Thomas, Isaiah 22

      Mass Moments. "Isaiah Thomas Born." <u>Massmoments.org</u>. Mass Humanities. Web.

Woman's Rights Convention 20

      Weatherford, Doris. "Timeline." A History of the American Suffragist Movement. Santa Barbara, CA: ABC-CLIO, 1998.
        <u>Suffragist.com</u>. The Moschovitis Group, Inc. Web.

GRAPHICS CREDITS - FIRST IN THE U.S.A. • People

Bancroft, George 23

      Klann, Ashley. Bancroft Tower. 2011. Photograph. Worcester, MA. <u>Clarknews.wordpress.com</u>. Clark University, 12 May 2011. Web.

      Photograph. Worcester Historical Museum, Worcester, MA.

Michelson, Albert A. 21

      Albert Michelson. Photograph. <u>Superstock.com</u>. SuperStock. Web.

      Fiorenza, Nick A. The Measurement of Light. <u>Lunarplanner.com</u>. Web.

Perkins, Frances 20

      Benoit, June. Photograph. Frances Perkins Library. 2012.

      Frances Perkins. Photograph. <u>Weeklyreader.com</u>. Weekly Reader Corporation. Web.

Reed, Chester A. 23

      Chester A. Reed. Photograph. Worcester Historical Museum, Worcester, MA.

      Photograph. Worcester Historical Museum, Worcester, MA.

Sampson, Deborah 21

      Deborah Sampson. Photograph. <u>Deborahsampsonpatriot.yolasite.com</u>. Yola. Web.

      Sharon Public Library. 2007. Photograph. Sharon, MA. <u>Zebwatersplace.blogspot.com</u>. Blogger. Web.

Spooner, Bathsheba 20

      Bathsheba Spooner. American Antiquarian Society, Worcester, MA.

Thomas, Isaiah 22

      Greenwood, Ethan A. Isaiah Thomas Sr. (1749-1831). 1818. Oil on panel. American Antiquarian Society, Worcester, MA.

Brinley Hall. Photograph. American Antiquarian Society, Worcester, MA. WWHP.org. Worcester Women's History Project. Web.

FIRST IN THE U.S.A. • Places

"Isaiah Thomas." Americanantiquarian.org. American Antiquarian Society, 22 Dec. 2009. Web.

Becking, Sarah H. "Isaiah Thomas and The Only Sure Guide to the English Tongue." Library.pitt.edu. University of Pittsburgh. Web.

Cataldo, Ashley. "Re: Final Edit of Text for Antiquarian." Message to the author. 30 Dec. 2011. E-mail.

McCorison, Marcus A., and John B. Hench. "A Brief History of the American Antiquarian Society." Americanantiquarian.org. American Antiquarian Society, 11 Mar. 2010. Web.

Terzian, Aved. "Re: Permission and Photo." Message to the author. 23 Dec. 2011. E-mail.

Rice, Franklin P. *Dictionary of Worcester (Massachusetts) and Its Vicinity.* Worcester, MA: F.S. Blanchard, 1893. Print.

Vartanian, Hrag. "The First Armenian American Communities Take Root: The Armenian American Plymouth." AGBU.org. Armenian General Benevolent Union, 3 Mar. 2001. Web.

Kalvinek, Patricia, and Robert C. Antonelli, Jr. "Re: Elm Park." Message to the author. 31 Jan. 2012. E-mail.

Miller, Michele. "17th Annual Elm Park Free Concert Series." Web log post. Activerain.com. ActiveRain Real Estate Network. Web.

Tulloch, Donald. *Worcester, City of Prosperity.* Worcester, MA: Commonwealth Press, 1914. Print.

"History of the Museum." Higgins.org. Higgins Armory Museum. Web.

Beeler, John H. "The John Woodman Higgins Armory." *Military Affairs*: 49.4 (1985): 198-202. Print.

Manahan, Janet. "FW: Monet." Message to the author. 10 Apr. 2012. E-mail.

Smee, Sebastian. "Worcester Art Museum, Poised for Change." Boston.com. The New York Times Company, 23 Oct. 2011. Web.

Welu, Jim. "Re: Pink Flamingo." Message to the author. 5 Mar. 2012. E-mail.

"Worcester Art Museum Acquires Recovered Pissarro Painting." Worcesterart.org. Worcester Art Museum, 9 Apr. 1999. Web.

Worcester State Hospital 25

Leas, Robert. "A Brief History of ACPE." ACPE.edu. The Association for Clinical Pastoral Education, Inc., 2008. Web.

Packard, Deborah, and Preservation Worcester. "Concerning the 'Environmental Notification Form – Worcester State Hospital Clock Tower Demolition.'" Letter to Richard K. Sullivan. 10 Jan. 2012. MS. Energy & Environmental Affairs, Boston.

GRAPHICS CREDITS - FIRST IN THE U.S.A. • Places

American Antiquarian Society 25

Exterior View of Antiquarian Hall. Photograph. Americanantiquarian.org. American Antiquarian Society. Web.

Photograph. American Antiquarian Society, Worcester, MA.
Printing Press. Photograph. American Antiquarian Society, Worcester, MA.

Holy Savior 24

Photograph. Armenian Church of Our Savior, Worcester, MA.

Elm Park 24

Photograph. Worcester Historical Museum, Worcester, MA.

Higgins Armory 25

Photograph. Higgins Armory, Worcester, MA.

Worcester Art Museum 25

Monet, Claude. Water Lilies. 1908. Oil on canvas. Worcester Art Museum, Worcester, MA.

Worcester State Hospital 25

Worcester State Hospital. 2005. Photograph. Opacity.us. Web.

FIRST IN THE U.S.A. • Space

Anti-G Suit 27

Barry, Daniel. "Re: Space Text for Book." Message to the author. 2 Feb. 2012. E-mail.

"David Clark Aerospace Products." Davidclark.com. David Clark Company, Inc. Web.

Messier, Doug. "USA, Moon Express and David Clark Company Join Commercial Spaceflight Federation." Parabolicarc.com. Parabolic Arc: 22 Sept. 2011. Web.

"Worcester and the National Space Program." Worcesterhistory.org. Worcester Historical Museum. Web.

Keogh, Jim. "From Clark to the Moon." Clark Alumni Magazine, Fall 2011: 14-21. Clarku.edu. Clark University. Web.

Clark University Archives. "The First Liquid-Fueled Rocket." Clarku.edu. Clark University. Web.

Clark University Archives. "Frequently Asked Questions About Dr. Robert H. Goddard." Clarku.edu. Clark University. Web.

Smithsonian National Air and Space Museum. "Milestones of Flight: Goddard Rockets." Nasm.si.edu. Smithsonian Institution. Web.

Williams, Fordyce. "Re: Archival Information on Clark." Message to the author. 25 July 2011. E-mail.

"David Clark Aerospace Products." Davidclark.com. David Clark Company, Inc. Web.

Donker, Peter P. "The Stars of Apollo." Honematic.com. Honematic Machine Corporation, 17 July 1994. Web.

Keogh, Jim. "From Clark to the Moon." Clark Alumni Magazine, Fall 2011: 14-21. Clarku.edu. Clark University. Web.

Barry, Daniel. "Re: Space Text for Book." Message to the author. 2 Feb. 2012. E-mail.

Donker, Peter P. "The Stars of Apollo." Honematic.com. Honematic Machine Corporation, 17 July 1994. Web.

"G4C." Astronautix.com. Encyclopedia Astronautica. Web.

GRAPHICS CREDITS - FIRST IN THE U.S.A. • Space

First Standard Anti-G Suits and Valves. Photograph. Davidclark.com. David Clark Company, Inc. Web.

Photograph. Clark University, Worcester, MA.

Photograph. Clark University, Worcester, MA.

FIRST IN THE U.S.A. • Sports

Taylor, Marshall "Major" **29**

Southwick, Albert B. *More Once-Told Tales of Worcester County.* Worcester, MA: Chandler House Press, 1994. Print.

Ritchie, Andrew. *Major Taylor: The Extraordinary Career of a Champion Bicycle Racer.* San Francisco: Bicycle, 1988. Print.

Tolman, Lynne. "Major Taylor - Biography at a Glance." Majortaylorassociation.org. The Major Taylor Association, Inc. Web.

Tolman, Lynne. "'Worcester Whirlwind' Overcame Bias." Majortaylorassociation.org. The Major Taylor Association, Inc., 23 July 1995. Web.

GRAPHICS CREDITS - FIRST IN THE U.S.A. • Sports

100-Mile Bike Race **28**

60770_boneshake. Etc.usf.edu. Florida Center for Instructional Technology. Web.

Candlepin Bowling **28**

Raymond, JeanPaul. Candlepin. 2012.

Curveball Pitch **29**

Candy Cummings. Photograph. Bleacherreport.com. Bleacher Report, Inc., 13 Feb. 2011. Web.

Raymond, JeanPaul. Shell. 2012.

Perfect Game **28**

Lee Richmond. Photograph. Writingqueen.wordpress.com. 2 July 2010. Web.

Ryder Cup **29**

Hagen, Walter. 1927 Ryder Cup. 1927. Photograph. Worcestercc.com. Worcester Country Club. Web.

Taylor, Marshall "Major" **29**

Marshall Taylor circa 1900. Photograph. The Burns Archive. Wikipedia.org. Wikimedia Foundation, Inc., 5 Feb. 2012.

Believe It or Not

Flies **30**

"$650 in Cash Prizes to 153 Winners!" *Worcester Daily Telegram*: 20 June 1911, XXVI ed. Print.

"Big Prizes for Children to Make Worcester First Flyless City in Country." *Evening Gazette* [Worcester, MA]: 19 June 1911, LXVIII ed. Print.

Williams, Fordyce. "Re: Research Question." Message to the author. 19 Jan. 2012. E-mail.

GRAPHICS CREDITS • Believe It or Not

Flies 30

"$650 in Cash Prizes to 153 Winners!" *Worcester Daily Telegram:* 20 June 1911, XXVI ed. Print.

"Big Prizes for Children to Make Worcester First Flyless City in Country." *Evening Gazette* [Worcester, MA]: 19 June 1911, LXVIII ed. Print.

Hodge, C. F. Photograph. "The Right Plan of Campaign for the War on the Fly on the Farm and in the City."
   Worcester, MA: *La Follette's Weekly*: 1912. Print.

"DO YOU KNOW...?"

S.1   **E. W. Vaill** 32

Washburn, Charles Grenfill. *Industrial Worcester*: Accessed through <u>books.google.com</u>. Google Books. Web.

E. W. Vaill folding chair advertisement, provided by Steven Rotman.

S.2   **Fenway Home Run** 32

Ballou, Bill. "Grafton's Hugh Bradley first over Green Monster." <u>Telegram.com</u>. Worcester Telegram & Gazette Corp., 20 Apr. 2012. Web.

S.3   **Robert Benchley** 32

"A City of Words: The Worcester Writers Project." WPI. Web. <u><http://users.wpi.edu/~cityofwords/benchley.html></u>

1.   **Esther Forbes** 34

Dictionary of Literary Biography. "Esther Forbes | Biography." <u>BookRags.com</u>. Thomson Gale, 2006. Web.

LeBarron, Michael, and Andrea Hubbard. "Esther Forbes." <u><Users.wpi.edu/~cityofwords/></u>. Worcester Polytechnic Institute, 2002. Web.

2.   **Ted Williams** 34

"Famous Firsts of Worcester, Mass." <u>Worcestermass.com</u>. Charles R. Grosvenor Jr. Web.

"Unique Central Massachusetts Facts." <u>Centralmass.org</u>. Central Massachusetts Convention and Visitors Bureau, 2011. Web.

3.   **Worcester Music Festival** 34

"About Us." <u>Musicworcester.org</u>. Music Worcester, Inc. Web.

Hovenesian, Stasia B. "Historical Data." Message to the author. 15 Nov. 2011. E-mail.

Sayers, Robin. "Denis Leary." LAtimesmagazine.com. Los Angeles Times Communications LLC: Aug. 2011. Web.

"Overview." The Leary Firefighters Foundation. www.learyfirefighters.org. Web.

Fano, Ellen. "Denis Leary." Message to the author. 4 June 2012. E-mail.

Hutchinson, Edward R. "Former Residents of Dewitt, NY - Circa 1940-1960 (V-Z)." ERHutchison.com. E. R. Hutchison, 2010. Web.

Reis, Jacqueline. "New North High Taking Shape." *Telegram & Gazette* [Worcester, MA]: 18 May 2011. Print.

"Who Is Abby Kelley Foster?" Abbyshouse.org. Abby Kelley Foster House, Inc. Web.

"Who Was Abby Kelley Foster?" WWHP.org. Worcester Women's History Project, 2012. Web.

Abramoff, Larry, Gloria Abramoff, and Ann Lindblad. *Favorite Places of Worcester County: A Guide to Shopping, Dining, Recreation, Sightseeing, History, Facts & Fun in Central Massachusetts.* Worcester, MA: Chandler House, 1999. Print.

"Edward Davis Jones." Riheritagehalloffame.org. Rhode Island Heritage Hall of Fame, 2011. Web.

"The Industrial Average Is Born: Co-created By Edward D. Jones." Investing-for-Beginner.org. 2011. Web.

Callahan, Frank. "Cole Porter at Worcester Academy." Wamash.worcesteracademy.org. Worcester Academy, 22 Jan. 2010. Web.

"WA Celebrating 175th Anniversary." Worcesteracademy.org. Worcester Academy, 24 Feb. 2009. Web.

Cinclair, Rick. "Andrew Haswell Green; Father of Greater New York." *Telegram & Gazette* [Worcester, MA]: 1 Mar. 2009. Thefreelibrary.com. Farlex, Inc. Web.

Sacks, Pamela H. "Green Estate Items to Be Auctioned at DCU Center." *Telegram & Gazette* [Worcester, MA]: 5 Sept. 2010. Print.

Abramoff, Larry, Gloria Abramoff, and Ann Lindblad. *Favorite Places of Worcester County: A Guide to Shopping, Dining, Recreation, Sightseeing, History, Facts & Fun in Central Massachusetts.* Worcester, MA: Chandler House, 1999. Print.

Goldman, Emma. "'I Will Kill Frick': Emma Goldman Recounts the Attempt to Assassinate the Chairman of the Carnegie Steel Company During the Homestead Strike in 1892." *Living My Life.* New York: Alfred Knopf, 1931. 83-88. Historymatters.gmu.edu. American Social History Productions, Inc. Web.

"People & Events: Henry Clay Frick (1849-1919)." PBS.org. PBS Online, 11 Mar. 2004. Web.

Ceccacci, Susan. Preservation Worcester. Telephone interview.

Christensen, Robyn. Worcester Historical Museum. "Emma Goldman." Message to the author. 13 Apr. 2012. E-mail.

If you have conclusive evidence of where Emma Goldman's ice cream parlor was located, we'd love to hear from you!

Abramoff, Larry, Gloria Abramoff, and Ann Lindblad. *Favorite Places of Worcester County: A Guide to Shopping, Dining, Recreation, Sightseeing, History, Facts & Fun in Central Massachusetts.* Worcester, MA: Chandler House, 1999. Print.

"Jack Smith." Referenceforbusiness.com. Advameg, Inc. Web.

Mashberg, Tom. "Command Change at General Motors, Worcester Native John Smith Alone at the Top; Dividend Cut 50 Percent." Boston Globe: 3 Nov. 1992. Highbeam.com. Cengage Learning. Web.

Everett, Otis W. Roller for Skates. Patent 823939. 19 June 1906. Print.

Everett, Otis W. Skate. Patent 690711. 7 Jan. 1902. Print.

Lambert, Luna. *The American Skating Mania: Ice Skating in the Nineteenth Century.* Washington: Smithsonian Institution, National Museum of History and Technology, 1978. Print.

White, Donald B. "Worcester Historical Society Receives Collection of 50 Ice and Roller Skates." *Worcester Daily Telegram* [Worcester, MA]: 25 Sept. 1959. Print.

"Winslow, Samuel Ellsworth-Biographical Information." Bioguide.congress.gov. Biographical Directory of the United States Congress. Web.

Office of Public Affairs. "UMass Medical School Professor Wins Nobel Prize." Umassmed.edu. University of Massachusetts, Worcester Campus, Oct. 2006. Web.

"The Nobel Prize in Physiology or Medicine 2006." Nobelprize.org. The Nobel Foundation, 2006. Web.

Arapoglou, Eleftheria. "Identity Configuration and Ideological Manipulation in Nicholas Gage's *A Place for Us.*" MELUS 30.3 (205): 71-93. JSTOR. Web. www.jstor.org.

Gage, Nicholas. *Eleni.* New York: Random House, 1983. Print.

Berg, Julia. "Nicholas Gage." <Users.wpi.edu/~cityofwords/>. Worcester Polytechnic Institute, 2009. Web.

40. Pipe Organ **43**

"Organs in the Movies." <u>Theatreorgans.com</u>. Web.

"The Bostonians: Did You Know?" <u>IMDb.com</u>. IMDb.com, Inc. Web.

41. Denholm's **44**

Sawyer, Christopher, and Patricia A. Wolf. *Denholm's: The Story of Worcester's Premier Department Store.* Charleston, SC: History, 2011. Print.

42. Worcester Lunch Car Company **44**

Fitzgerald, Craig. "Worcester Lunch Car Company." *Hemmings Motor News* [Bennington, VT]: Dec. 2008. <u>Hemmings.com</u>. American City Business Journals. Web.

Harris, Patricia, and David Lyon. "Ten Diners Stamped 'Worcester.'" <u>Boston.com</u>. New York Times Company, 7 Mar. 2010. Web.

"Restaurants." <u>Holycross.edu</u>. College of the Holy Cross. Web.

43. Infamous Bank Robber **44**

"Echoes From the Past: Worcester Criminals; Sponsored by Worcester Historical Museum." Advertisement. <u>Artsboston.org</u>. ArtsBoston, Apr. 2012. Web.

Rushford, David J. "Trivia - Famous People & Events." <u>Worcesterma.gov</u>. City of Worcester, MA. Web.

44. Rolling Stones **45**

"20,000 Lightyears From Boston." <u><Luckydogmusic.com/rolling.html></u>. Lucky Dog Music Hall, 11 Jan. 2003. Web.

45. Fixed the *Massachusetts Spy* Press **45**

Nylander, Holly K. *History of Worcester, MA: 1880 to 1920.* Worcester, MA: Preservation Worcester. Print.

Rushford, David J. "Trivia - Famous People & Events." <u>Worcesterma.gov</u>. City of Worcester, MA. Web.

46. Phil Bissell **45**

Langone, Matt. "Bissell and His Legendary 'Pat Patriot' Logo Celebrate 50 Years." <u>Salemnews.com</u>. Community Newspaper Holdings, Inc., 28 Aug. 2009. Web.

Langone, Matt. "The Return of Pat Patriot." <u>Eagletribune.com</u>. Community Newspaper Holdings, Inc., 2 Sept. 2009. Web.

47. Michael McGrath **46**

"Worcester's Michael McGrath Snares Honor at Tony Awards." *Telegram & Gazette* [Worcester, MA]: 11 June 2012. <u>Telegram.com</u>. Web.

Fano, Ellen. "Worcester's Michael McGrath snares honor at Tony Awards." Message to the author. 13 June 2012. E-mail.

"Worcester Three-decker Survey." Clark University Graduate School of Geography, February 1981.

McEttrick, Jacqui and Philip Schneider. "Worcester's Three-deckers."
<http://college.holycross.edu/projects/worcester/immigration/3deckers.htm>. College of the Holy Cross. Web.

Hennessy, Dennis. Worcester Economic Development. Telephone interview, 16 July 2012.

Kush, Bronislaus B. "Three-decker Threat: Iconic Structures Placed on List for Preservation." Telegram.com.
Worcester Telegram & Gazette Corp., 25 Mar. 2012. Web.

"1919 Ad M. J. Whittall Woven Oriental Rugs Worcester - Original Print Ad."
<www.amazon.com/1919-Whittall-Woven-Oriental-Worcester/dp/B005DH4G6E. Amazon.com>. Web.

"Matthew J. Whittall." <www.prospectfriends.org/History.html>. Friends of Prospect Park, Inc. Web.

Wallace, William D. "Questions for Bill Wallace." Message to the author. 13 July 2012. E-mail.

"DO YOU KNOW...?" • ANSWERS & GRAPHICS CREDITS

"Folding Chair" - Indianapolis Museum of Art: http://www.imamuseum.org/art/collections/artwork/folding-chair--0

Photograph. www.baseballreference.com. Web. http://www.baseball-reference.com/players/b/bradlhu01.shtml

Jaws Movie Poster. Universal Pictures. Content is available under Creative Commons Attribution-Share Alike License 3.0 (Unported) (CC-BY-SA).
Web. http://horror-movies.wikia.com/wiki/File:Jaws-movie-poster_%281%29.jpg#filelinks

Raymond, JeanPaul. Johnny Tremain. 2012. Worcester, MA.

Photograph courtesy of Daniel Higgins. 1939. Worcester, MA.

Worcester Autographs